AF879394

AI Literacy Courseware
English

Colophon

Title:	AI Literacy Courseware - English
Authors:	Rowel Gündlach Sophie Campman
Publisher:	Van Haren Publishing, 's-Hertogenbosch
ISBN Paperback:	978 94 018 1390 7
Edition:	First edition, first print, November, 2025
Design:	Van Haren Publishing, 's-Hertogenbosch
Copyright:	© Van Haren Publishing 2025

For further information about Van Haren Publishing please e-mail us at: info@vanharen.net or visit our website: www.vanharen.net

Publisher about the Courseware

The Courseware was created by experts from the industry who served as the author(s) for this publication. The input for the material is based on existing publications and the experience and expertise of the author(s). The material has been revised by trainers who also have experience working with the material. Close attention was also paid to the key learning points to ensure what needs to be mastered.

The objective of the courseware is to provide maximum support to the trainer and to the student, during his or her training. The material has a modular structure and according to the author(s) has the highest success rate should the student opt for examination. The Courseware is also accredited for this reason, wherever applicable.

In order to satisfy the requirements for accreditation the material must meet certain quality standards. The structure, the use of certain terms, diagrams and references are all part of this accreditation. Additionally, the material must be made available to each student in order to obtain full accreditation. To optimally support the trainer and the participant of the training assignments, practice exams and results are provided with the material.

Direct reference to advised literature is also regularly covered in the sheets so that students can find additional information concerning a particular topic. The decision to leave out notes pages from the Courseware was to encourage students to take notes throughout the material. Although the courseware is complete, the possibility that the trainer deviates from the structure of the sheets or chooses to not refer to all the sheets or commands does exist. The student always has the possibility to cover these topics and go through them on their own time. It is recommended to follow the structure of the courseware and publications for maximum exam preparation.

The courseware and the recommended literature are the perfect combination to learn and understand the theory.

-- Van Haren Publishing

Other publications BY Van Haren Publishing

Van Haren Publishing (VHP) specializes in titles on Best Practices, methods, frameworks and standards within four domains:
- IT Management
- Architecture (Enterprise and IT)
- Business Management and
- Project Management

Van Haren Publishing is publishing on behalf of leading organizations and companies: Agile Consortium, World Commerce and Contracting, IAOP, IPMA World, KNVI, PMI-NL, NLAIC and The Open Group.

Van Haren Publishing is part of the Van Haren Group and additional to the book publishing also provides the following services: accredited training materials and e-learning through Van Haren Learning Solutions, as well as independent professional certification via examination through Van Haren Certify.

Topics are (per domain):

IT Management	IT Service Management	FitSM, ISM®, ISO/IEC20000, IT4IT®, ITIL®, VerISM®, SAF, TRIM, XLA®
	Data Management	Data literacy, Data visualization, DMBOK
	IT Asset Management	HAM, ITAM, SAM
	IT Security Management	BIO, ISO/IEC27001, NIS2
	Test Management	CTAP
	Application Management	ASL
	Other	eCF, IT-CMF, Scrum
Project Management	Project Management	Half Double, ICB, ISO/IEC21500, P3.express, PM2, PMBOK Guide, Praxis, PRINCE2
	Agile	Agile, Agile PM
	Other	PMO
Business Management	Operations Management	Lean, Lean Six Sigma, OBM, OMC, RASCI
	Contract Management	CATS CM, CATS RVM, IACCM World
	Business Information Management	BiSL, DID
	Artificial Intelligence	AI, Generative AI
	Outsourcing	OPBOK
Enterprise Architecture	Enterprise Architecture	BIAN, TOGAF
	Modeling	ArchiMate, BPMN
	Software Architecture	ISAQB
	Other	Open Agile Architecture

For the latest information on VHP publications, visit our website: www.vanharen.net.

Table of Content

Self-Reflection of understanding Diagram

'What you do not measure, you cannot control.'' – Tom Peters

Fill in this diagram to self-evaluate your understanding of the material. This is an evaluation of how well you know the material and how well you understand it. In order to pass the exam successfully you should be aiming to reach the higher end of Level 3. If you really want to become a pro, then you should be aiming for Level 4. Your overall level of understanding will naturally follow the learning curve. So, it's important to keep track of where you are at each point of the training and address any areas of difficulty.

Based on where you are within the Self-Reflection of Understanding diagram you can evaluate the progress of your own training.

Level of Understanding	Before Training (Pre-knowledge)	Training Part 1 (1st Half)	raining Part 2 (2nd Half)	After studying / reading the book	After exercises and the Practice exam
Level 4 ***I can explain the content and apply it .***					
Level 3 I get it! ***I am right where I am supposed to be.***					Ready for the exam!
Level 2 ***I almost have it but could use more practice.***					
Level 1 ***I am learning but don't quite get it yet.***					

(Self-Reflection of Understanding Diagram)

Write down the problem areas that you are still having difficulty with so that you can consolidate them yourself, or with your trainer. After you have had a look at these, then you should evaluate to see if you now have a better understanding of where you actually are on the learning curve.

Troubleshooting

Problem areas:	***Topic:***
Part 1	
Part 2	
You have gone through the book and studied.	
You have answered the questions and done the practice exam.	

Agenda	
09:00 – 10:00:	An introduction to AI
09:00 – 10:00:	Break
10:10 – 11:00:	Data and AI: How it works and its challenges
11:00 – 11:10:	Break
11:10 – 12:00:	Data and AI: How it works and its challenges
12:00 – 13:00:	Break
13:00 – 14:00:	Opportunities and challenges of AI in your work
14:00 – 14:10:	Break
14:10 – 15:00:	Opportunities and challenges of AI in your work
15:00 – 15:10:	Break
15:10 – 16:15:	Ethics and regulation

AI Literacy

Introduction

Who are you?

- Name & role
- Do you already encounter AI (at work or in daily life)
- What would you like to get out of this training?

 2

The European AI Act, the reason we are here

- First comprehensive **law** in the world regulating Artificial Intelligence (AI)
- Classifies AI systems by **risk level**
- Sets rules for trustworthy AI in the EU
- Aimed at **developers, deployers, and users** of AI
- States that users of AI should be AI-literate

 3

What does this mean for you?

- Dutch companies and public organizations must **comply with EU standards**
- Citizens will **interact more often with AI systems** in work, education, and daily life
- Growing demand for **AI understanding and responsible use** across all roles
- Need to recognize **bias, misinformation, and automation risks**
- AI literacy helps individuals **use AI safely and ethically** under the new regulations

 4

Levels of AI literacy

- There are different **levels of data and AI literacy**, as defined by the Dutch government
  - Not every employee interacts with data and AI in the same way or with the same intensity
  - The expected skills and knowledge about data and AI vary by role and responsibility
  - There is a wide range of prior knowledge, some employees may have studied analytical topics or read about data-driven work, while others have little or no exposure to the subject

Levels of AI and data literacy and their core focus

1. Data and AI **aware**	2. Data and AI **proficient**	3. Data and AI **fluent**	4. Data and AI **expert**
Basic knowledge and awareness of AI and data	Critical application and evaluation of AI and analyses. Basic knowledge of data collection.	In-depth understanding and knowledge of working with data & AI, the prerequisites, and the opportunities.	Designing, developing, and optimizing data and AI solutions.

Levels and core focus as described by the Dutch government data and AI literacy working group.

After today you will be ...

1. Data and AI aware

Basic knowledge and awareness of AI and data

2. Data and AI proficient

Critical application and evaluation of AI and analyses. Basic knowledge of data collection.

3. Data and AI fluent

In depth understanding and knowledge of working with data & AI, the prerequisites, and the opportunities.

4. Data and AI expert

Designing, developing and optimizing data and AI solutions.

Levels and core focus as described by the Dutch government data and AI literacy working group.

 7

Core competences

1. Data and AI aware

1. Basic **knowledge** of common concepts related to data and AI
2. Ability to **recognize data** and **AI applications** in work processes
3. Understanding the **limitations** and **ethical considerations** of using data and AI
4. Ability to **work with** readily available **AI** and **data tools**

2. Data and AI proficient

1. Critical **evaluation** of **AI output** and data insights
2. Understanding how data and AI **support** and **influence decisions** in the organization, and the role they play in work and daily tasks
3. Ability to **identify opportunities** for using data and AI tools, formulate tasks and develop solutions
4. Basic knowledge of **AI and data risks** as well as **ethical issues** within the organization

 8

Learning objectives

After today, you will be able to...

- Understand **common terms** related to data and AI
- Understand that AI is a **tool** and not a definitive authority
- **Critically** assess the **output** generated by AI systems
- Recognize where AI and data **applications** are present in your work and daily tasks
- Understand how AI and data **support** and influence your work and daily tasks
- Identify **opportunities** for using data and AI tools, formulate clear tasks, and facilitate the development of solutions within your organization
- Understand **limitations** and **ethical challenges** associated with using AI
- **Effectively** and **correctly** work and interact with **readily available AI** and data tools

 9

Content overview

Part 1 – An introduction to AI

- What is AI?
- Why AI literacy?
- The origins of AI

Part 2 – Data and AI: How it works and its challenges

- Data and data quality
- The basic workings of AI

 10

Content overview

Part 3 – Opportunities and challenges of AI in your work

- Using AI in practice – output
- Using AI in practice – input

Part 4 – Ethics and regulation

- Ethical considerations related to using AI
- The European AI act
- The future of AI

Take home message

Agenda

- **09:00 – 10:00 > An introduction to AI**
- 10:00 – 10:10 > Break 01 (10 min)
- **10:10 – 11:00 > Data and AI: How it works and its challenges**
- 11:00 – 11:10 > Break 02 (10 min)
- **11:10 – 12:00 > Data and AI: How it works and its challenges**
- 12:00 – 13:00 > Break (60 min)
- **13:00 – 14:00 > Opportunities and challenges of AI in your work**
- 14:00 – 14:10 > Break 03 (10 min)
- **14:10– 15:00 > Opportunities and challenges of AI in your work**
- 15:00 – 15:10 > Break 04 (10 min)
- **15:10– 16:15 > Ethics and regulation**

Part 1 – An introduction to AI

Core competences addressed in Part 1

1. **Basic knowledge** of common concepts related to data and AI

What is AI?

From mind to math - the inspiration for AI

Source: Xkcd https://xkcd.com/435/

The definition of Intelligence

Intelligence can be defined as the ability to perceive or infer **information**, and to retain it as **knowledge** to be applied towards adaptive **behaviors** within an environment or context.

Artificial Intelligence (AI) can be defined as intelligence exhibited by **machines** with cognitive functions that are associated to humans.

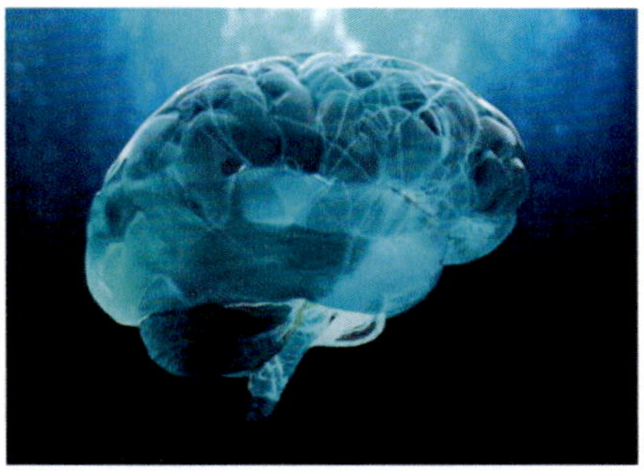

The concept of AI

- AI helps machines perform tasks that typically require **human intelligence**, e.g.,
  - Understanding language
  - Recognizing images or sounds
  - Learning from data
  - Solving problems
  - Interacting with people (e.g., chatbots)
- AI learns from data
  - AI learns from examples and experiences, not from fixed rules
  - AI recognizes patterns

The concept of AI

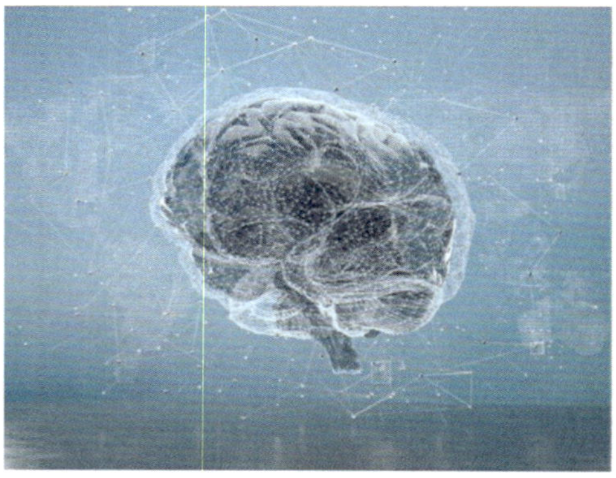

 19

Why AI literacy?

 20

AI literacy

- It helps you **understand** and **effectively** use AI
- It enables you to recognize **bias**
- It helps you to think **critically** about AI and its ethical implications
- It enables you to use AI **consciously** and **responsibly**

The European AI Act

Article 4 of the EU AI act reads

"Providers and deployers of AI systems shall take measures to ensure, to their best extent, a sufficient level of AI literacy of **their staff and other persons dealing with the operation and use of AI systems** on their behalf, taking into account their technical knowledge, experience, education and training and the context the AI systems are to be used in, and considering the persons or groups of persons on whom the AI systems are to be used."

The European AI Act

Article 4 of the EU AI act reads

"Providers and deployers of AI systems shall take measures to ensure, to their best extent, a sufficient level of AI literacy of **their staff and other persons dealing with the operation and use of AI systems** on their behalf, taking into account their technical knowledge, experience, education and training and the context the AI systems are to be used in, and considering the persons or groups of persons on whom the AI systems are to be used."

Since 2 February 2025: **mandatory** to be AI literate ⇒ **This training!**

The origins of AI

How did we get where we are now?

The history of AI

Inspiration

- In the late 19th century, people began to understand more about human biology

The start of AI

- 1950s: The birth of the concept of AI

AI in the fifties – The Turing test

- Alan Turing published an important paper in 1950 in which he speculates about the possibility of creating machines that think
- While the basic concepts of AI are still in their early stages, he devises his famous Turing test

The Turing test is a test of a machine's ability to exhibit intelligent behavior that is indistinguishable from that of a human.

The person in the middle has to identify who is the computer and who is the human. If they fail, the Turing test is passed

The history of AI

Inspiration

- In the late 19th century, people began to understand more about human biology

The start of AI

- 1950s: The birth of the concept of AI
- 1960s: Disappointing results, little development
- 1990s: Machines start to improve at games (checkers, chess)
- 2000s: Smart machines begin to make our lives easier
- 2010s: Big data, cloud, open source

 27

The current landscape of AI - upwards spiral

A Major Step for AI: Generative AI

- Since 2022, everyone has access to ChatGPT
- Rapid growth of generative AI

The successes of AI inspire more entities to develop and implement AI

- Companies invest in AI
- Students study and work in AI
- More technological advances in AI
- Companies invest more in AI
- ...

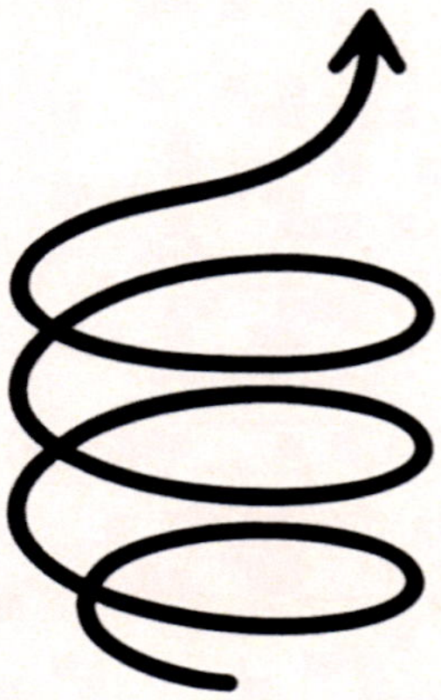

 28

Why now

Due to recent technological advances, we were able to make significant steps in the field of AI. The main contributing factors are

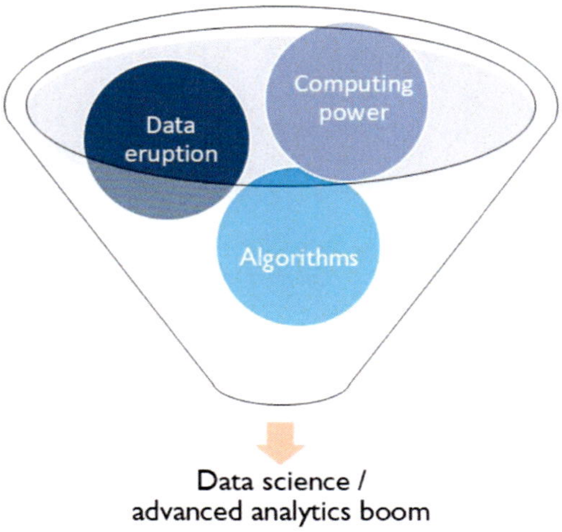

Data eruption

- More data available
- More storage capacity

Computing power

- Stronger CPU / GPU

Advanced algorithms

- Smarter mathematical models make AI stronger and more efficient

AI as the fourth industrial revolution

First (18th and 19th centuries)

- **Steam engine**

Second (1870 to 1914)

- **Electricity** (telephone, light bulb)

Third (1980s)

- Digital and **ICT** (information and communications technology)(personal computers, internet, automation)

Fourth (today)

- Exploits the digital revolution and is disruptive, driven by **AI**, robotics, Internet of Things, 3D printing, nanotech, bio-engineering.

The Fourth Industrial Revolution is changing every area of our lives.
Klaus Schwab – Founder of the World Economic Forum

Part 2 – Data and AI: How it works and its challenges

 31

Core competences addressed in Part 2

1. **Basic knowledge** of common concepts related to data and AI
2. Ability to **recognize data** and **AI applications** in work processes

 32

Data and data quality

 33

Data, Information, Knowledge and Intelligence

- **Data**:
  - raw building blocks, numbers without context
- **Information**:
  - structure or order in data
- **Knowledge**:
  - understanding of the information
- **Intelligence**:
  - Ability to use the information to make decisions
    - Recognize objects and events
    - Present knowledge in a real-world model
    - Reason about the future

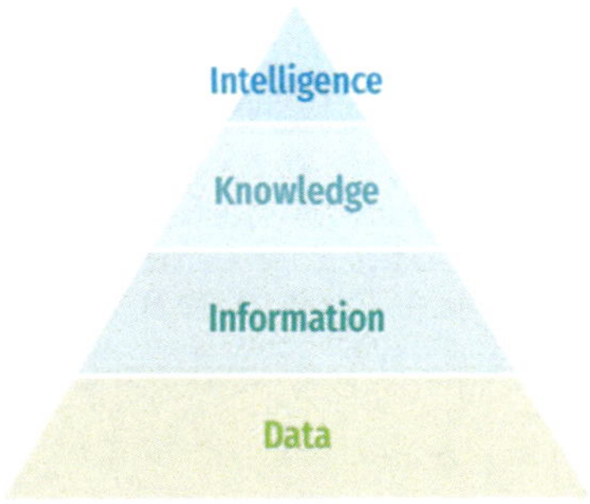

 34

Data, Information, Knowledge and Intelligence - Example

- **Data**: 24, 25, 25, 26, 28, 28, 30
- **Information**:

9:00	10:00	11:00	12:00	13:00	14:00	15:00
24°C	25°C	25°C	26°C	28°C	28°C	30°C

- **Knowledge**: It is getting warmer
- **Intelligence**: I should turn on the AC!

- **In practice, 'information' is also often called 'data'** (and we will do so from now on)

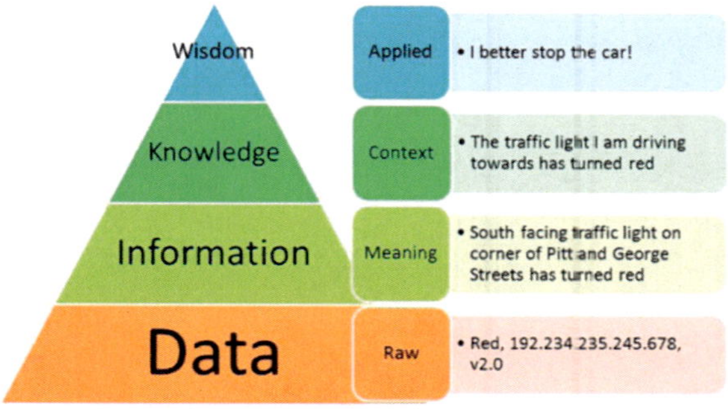

© Van Haren Publishing BV. 35

Unstructured vs structured data

Unstructured

The university has 5600 students.
John's ID is number 1, he is 18 years old and already holds a B.Sc. degree.
David's ID is number 2, he is 31 years old and holds a Ph.D. degree. Robert's ID is number 3, he is 51 years old and also holds the same degree as David, a Ph.D. degree.

Semi-structured

```
<University>
  <Student ID="1">
    <Name>John</Name>
    <Age>18</Age>
    <Degree>B.Sc.</Degree>
  </Student>
  <Student ID="2">
    <Name>David</Name>
    <Age>31</Age>
    <Degree>Ph.D. </Degree>
  </Student>
  ....
</University>
```

Structured

ID	Name	Age	Degree
1	John	18	B.Sc.
2	David	31	Ph.D.
3	Robert	51	Ph.D.
4	Rick	26	M.Sc.
5	Michael	19	B.Sc.

Source: https://www.researchgate.net/publication/236860222_Developing_Dynamic_Packaging_Applications_using_Semantic_Web_based_Integration

© Van Haren Publishing BV. 36

Types of Data

- **Structured data:** stored in a particular, well-defined format, fit for analysis as is:
  - Numbers, table, an Excel sheet
- **Unstructured data:** no predefined specific data model that all data points will adhere to:
  - Text, video, audio, internet content
  - Note: unstructured data is not immediately suitable for analysis
- **Semi-structured data:** no fixed data model, but metadata indicates contents:
  - JSON, XML are well known examples
  - Metadata gives semantic meaning to data:
    { "fruit": "banana", "color": "red" }
    { "fruit": "apple", "country": "Belgium" }

Big data

Big Data is the ocean of information we swim in every day – vast zettabytes of data flowing from our computers, mobile devices, and machine sensors.

Big data refers to **large and complex datasets** that cannot be easily processed using traditional data processing techniques. These datasets often include data from a variety of sources, such as social media, sensor data, and transactional data.

This data is used by organizations to drive decisions, improve processes and policies, and create customer-centric products, services, and experiences.

Data quality

- Data is the key driving force for AI
- Based on existing data, an **algorithm** finds certain patterns that is used to make future predictions

We make two key observations

- To make accurate predictions, an algorithm needs to find complex patterns in the data, which it only can when there is a large amount of data available
- The quality of the predictions depends on the quality of the data
- An algorithm can get stuck in a certain pattern

Data quality rule of thumb

The result of a machine learning algorithm is, at most, as good as the data that it uses

- Bad data = Bad results
- However, getting "good" data can be challenging

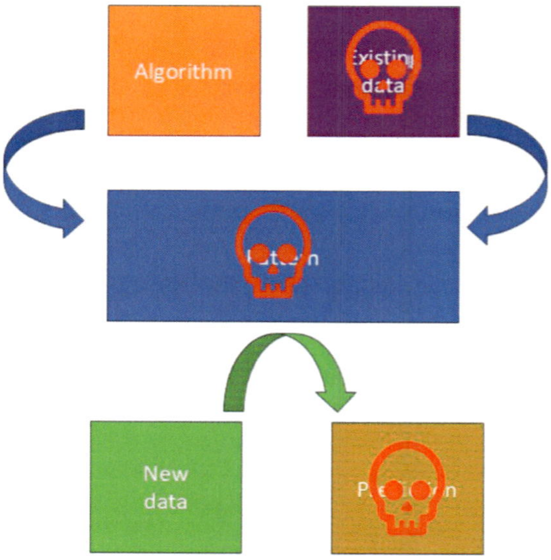

Challenge - Accuracy

Is it correct?

- Distribution of age

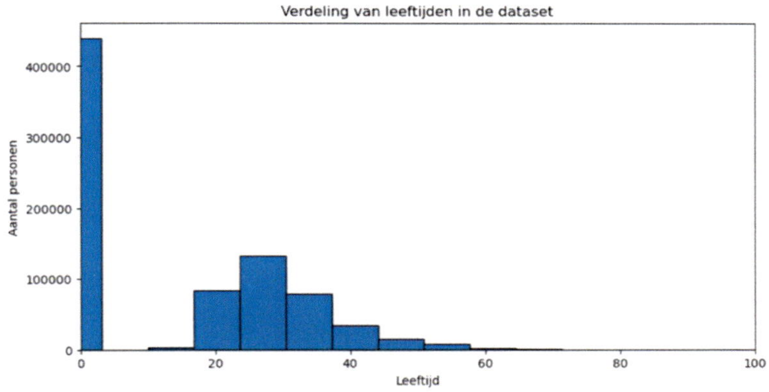

Sometimes data fields are not filled in and get a 0 by default. If this is not noticed, one may make predictions based on people with an age of 0!

 41

Challenge - Human error

Is it correct?

- Distribution of age
- Addresses

ID	Owner	City	Zip code
1	D. de Jong	Groningen	9718 AC
2	M. Bas	Amsterdam	1011 NK
3	D. de Waard	Groningen	9718 AC
4	S. van Houten	Eindhoven	1556 PE

When it comes to manually inserting data (for example zip codes) it is very easy to make a mistake. Eindhoven has a region code of 56, so there was a typo, but this is not easy to notice.

 42

Challenge - Uniqueness

- Is it free from duplication?

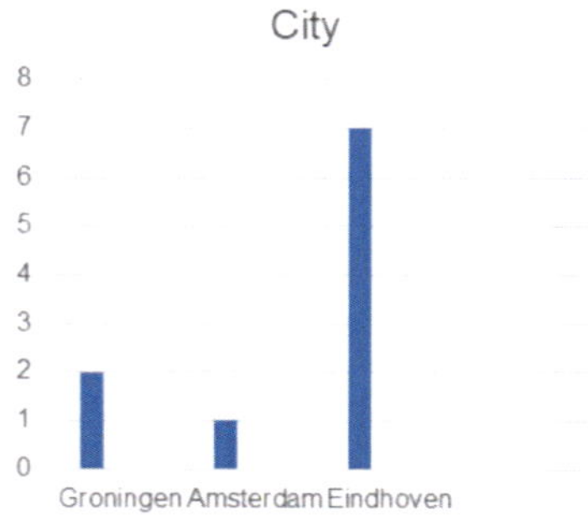

ID	Owner	City	Zip code
1	D. de Jong	Groningen	9718 AC
2	M. Bas	Amsterdam	1011 NK
3	D. de Waard	Groningen	9718 AC
4	S v houten	Eindhoven	1556 PE
5	S v houten	Eindhoven	5615 PE
6	S van houten	Eindhoven	5615 PE
7	S van Houten	Eindhoven	5615 PE
8	S. van Houten	Eindhoven	5615 PE

Duplication can introduce bias. In this example one may think the majority of the owners are from Eindhoven. However, identifying duplicates can sometimes be challenging (for example two of the exact same transaction that are made 2 seconds after each other

 43

Challenge - Automated data collection

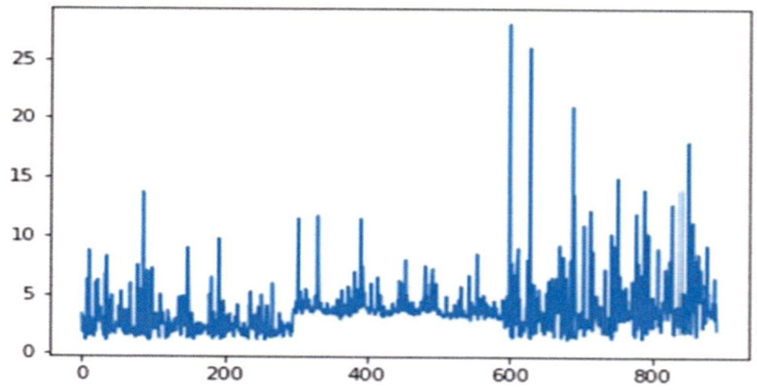

Sometimes unforeseen factors can break a stable trend in a process. For example, when an airco breaks for an hour, the temperature can systematically rise for a certain period of time. However, this behavior is typically not what we want to include in our analysis

 44

The basic workings of AI

Techniques

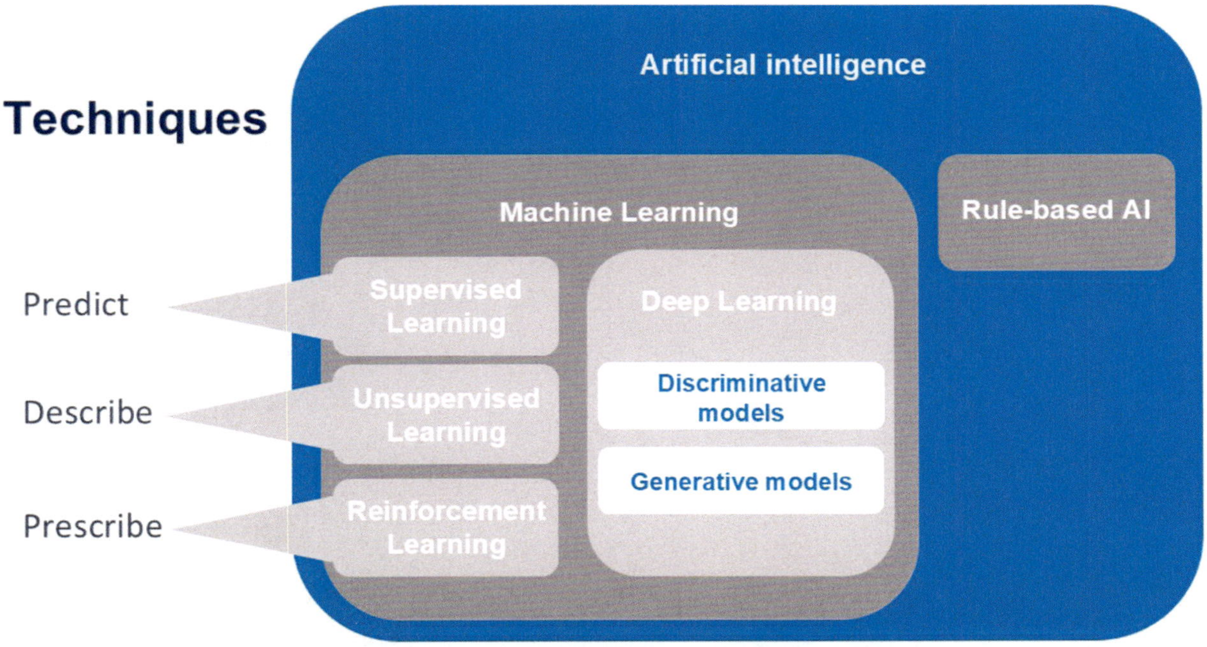

Machine learning definition

Tom Mitchell's definition is widely quoted:

"the field of machine learning is concerned with the question of how to construct computer programs that automatically ***improve with experience****."*

"a computer program is said to learn from experience, E*, with respect to some class of tasks,* T*, and performance measure,* P*, if its performance at tasks,* T*, as measured by* P*, improves with experience,* E*."*

 47

Machine learning models

Machine learning models combine **algorithms** (mathematical techniques) in combination with **existing data** to make predictions, such as:

- The answer to a question (ChatGPT)
- The likelihood of someone committing fraud
- If this object is a dog or a cat

Existing data contains hidden patterns
Algorithms uncovers hidden patterns in an efficient manner

Idea: Uncover hidden patterns based on existing data, then use this pattern to predict based on **new** data

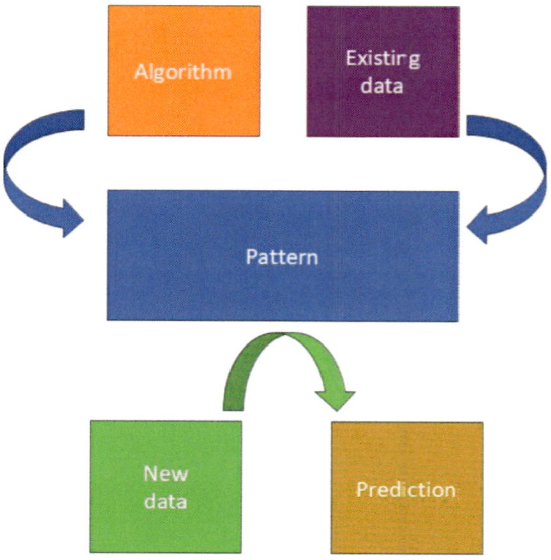

 48

Machine learning models - Example

Goal: Predict if a customer is going to pay back a loan

Existing data: Data of past customer, indicating who has and who has not paid back their loans

Algorithm: I look at 5 people in my data set that most closely resemble the current customer, if the majority has paid back their loan, I approve the loan

New data: A new customer comes in, I note all properties of this customer

Prediction: Based on the previously defined algorithm, I approve the loan or not

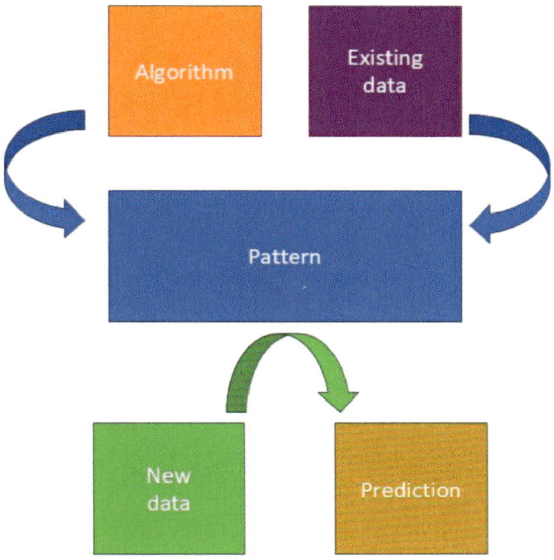

 49

Machine learning models - Exercise

For the following applications think of how AI can be used to analyze the following

- Use AI to increase customer satisfaction
- Use AI to when to do car maintenance
- Use AI to determine which places in the city need cleaning

Find what is the:
Existing data:
Algorithm: [Done by the trainer]
New data:
Prediction:

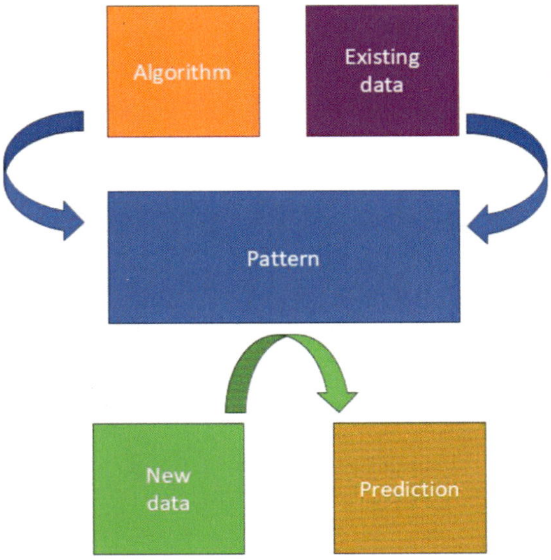

 50

Correlation and causation

Be careful how to interpret such a pattern!

- Correlation means that **a relation between two variables** exists
  - Positive correlation: if X is bigger, then Y is also bigger
  - Negative correlation: if X is bigger, then Y is smaller
- Causation is when **one event leads to another**
  - If X happens, then Y is also more likely because X can cause Y to happen

Correlation **does not mean** causation: cause and effect are often influenced by other variables.

Machine learning will never tell you a causal relationship, only correlations!

© Van Haren Publishing BV. 51

Prediction (supervised learning)

Based on past data AI can recognize certain **patterns** in the data to **predict** a certain outcome

- Predicting sales
- Spam filtering
- Fraud detection
- Predicting potential crime
- Predicting optimal candidates for a position
- Predicting health based on x-ray images

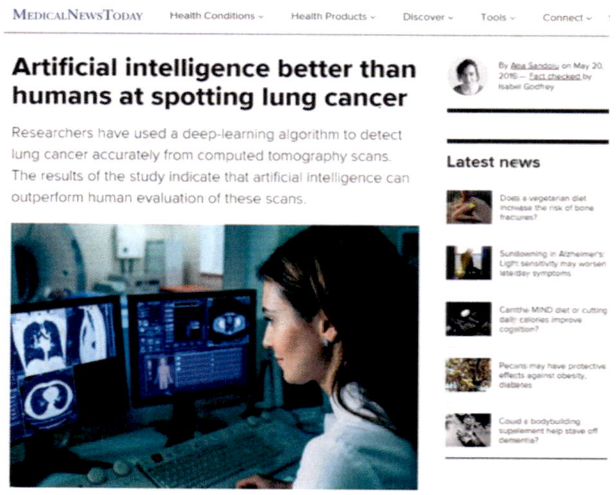
MEDICALNEWSTODAY Health Conditions Health Products Discover Tools Connect

Artificial intelligence better than humans at spotting lung cancer

Researchers have used a deep-learning algorithm to detect lung cancer accurately from computed tomography scans. The results of the study indicate that artificial intelligence can outperform human evaluation of these scans.

Latest news

© Van Haren Publishing BV. 52

Prediction (supervised learning)

A typical data set used to make predictions, contain

- Labels: The outcome, **the property you want to predict,** for example:
    - How many sales are we going to make?
    - Is this a fraudulent transaction?
    - Is this a healthy lung or not?
- Features: The information, **the properties that you know,** for example
    - What is the weather, which day of the week is it ...
    - What is the transaction amount, to which country is the transaction...
    - Which parts of the X-ray picture are which color ...

Description (unsupervised learning)

Based on data, AI can find **clusters** in data of objects that typically occur together

- Customer segmentation
- Anomaly detection
- Market basket analysis

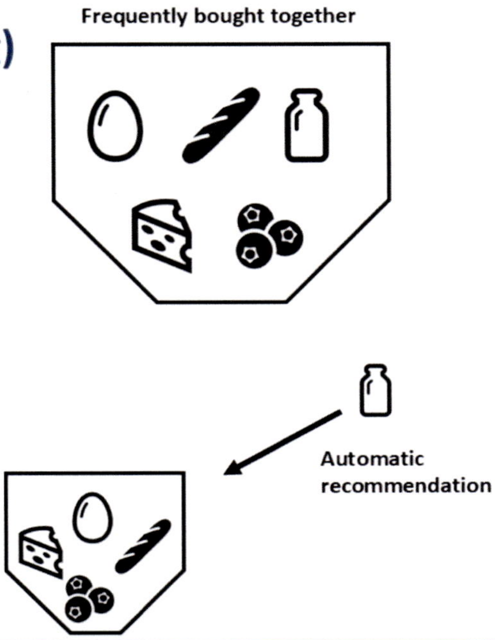

Prescription (reinforcement learning)

Based on data, AI can **learn** from decisions that it makes, where it can either be rewarded or punished via (human) feedback, so that it will always choose actions that maximize its rewards

- Optimal maintenance strategies
- Investment strategies
- Dynamic pricing
- Playing games

This is typically a computationally heavy approach in machine learning

 55

General object detection

Based on data (images) AI can **identify** what a typical object looks like and recognize this in new images

- Quick and real-time detection of any object
- Allows machines to recognize objects and interact with them
- Useful in video surveillance
- But can struggle with unusual objects
- Requires many images of the object in order recognize it

Detecting different types of trash on the street

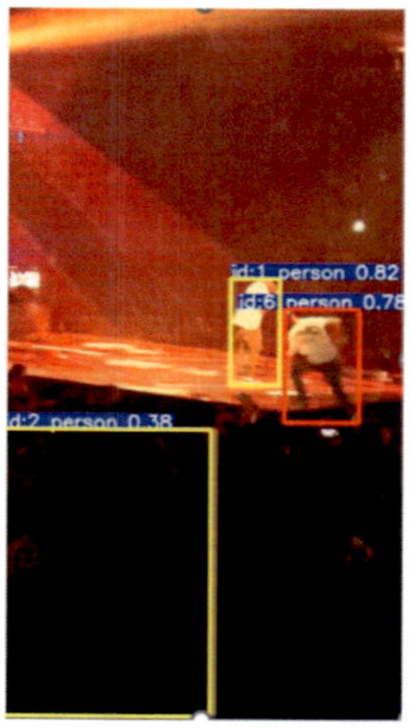

Detecting disruptions at concerts

 56

Generative AI (GenAI)

AI can **create** new and "original" content, like images, music and texts based on algorithms and models, based on existing training data.

- Text (ChatGPT and Copilot)
- Images
- Videos
- Music

 57

Machine learning models – Neural networks

Algorithms are in practice very complex, the most used example is a neural network

- Inspired by the human brain
- Are widely used in many AI applications, such as ChatGPT
- Contain many complex mathematical structures

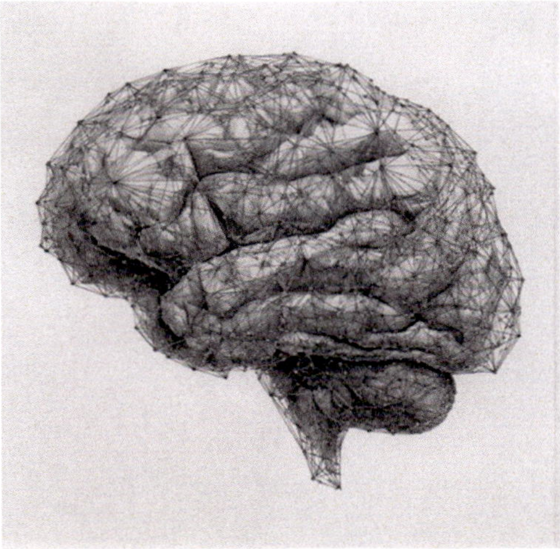

 58

Neural Networks

Neural networks for number detection

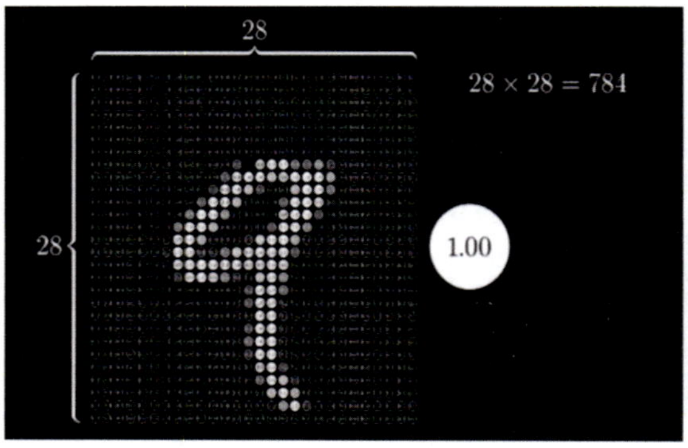

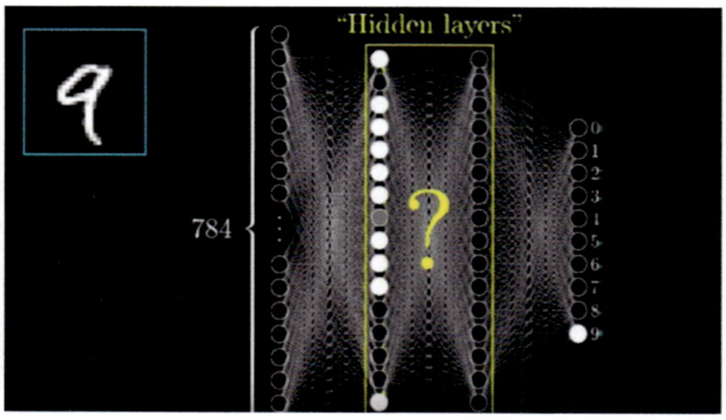

https://www.linkedin.com/pulse/machine-learning-how-does-neural-network-recognize-digits-wallace/

 59

Neural Networks

Neural networks for number detection

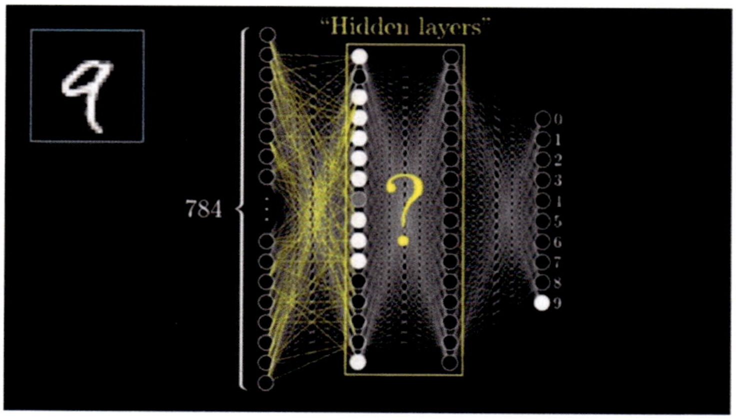

https://www.linkedin.com/pulse/machine-learning-how-does-neural-network-recognize-digits-wallace/

 60

Explainability of AI

While neural networks are strong models in practice, they have some major downsides

Explainability means that it is **unclear** why AI has made a certain prediction

- You know which neurons were activated but that does not tell you anything about the pattern
- While in theory you could post-hoc explain what the function of a certain neuron is, this is not reasonable in practice
- This makes it a **black box model**

There are forms of AI that are **white box models,** but they are often less powerful. We see the impact of this later in the training

AI in everyday life

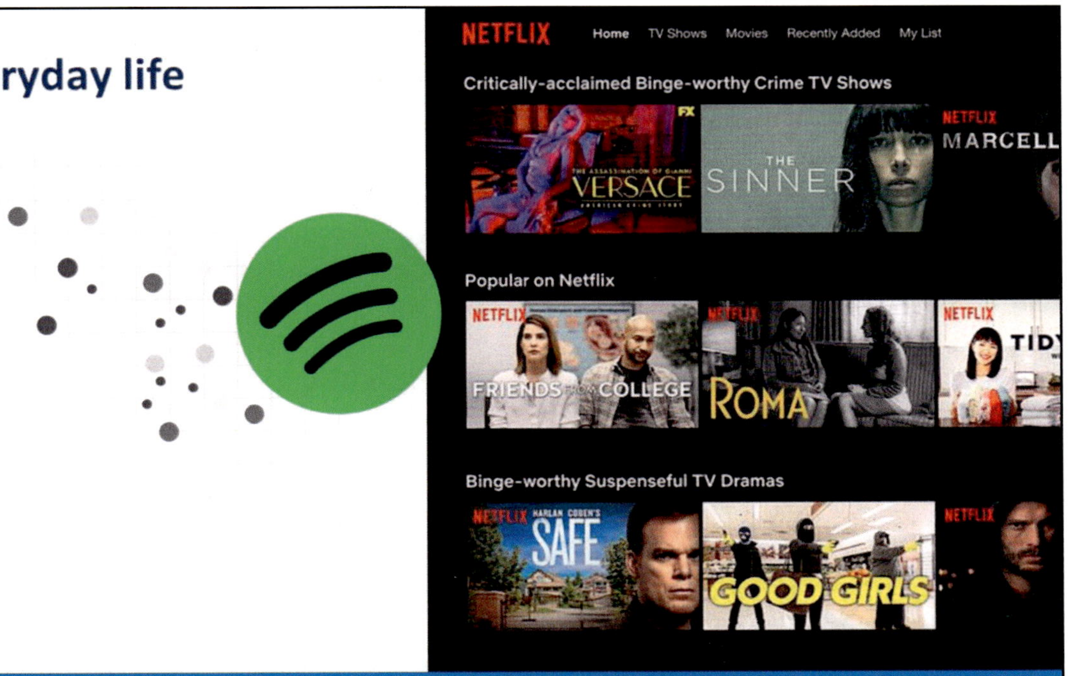

AI in everyday life

 63

Case study – Crime prediction

- Dutch police forces are using AI to predict criminal behavior on a large scale in the Netherlands
- This system is called CAS (Criminaliteits Anticipatie Systeem)

Predictive policing of the Dutch police

- Based on a grid, an algorithm predicts the probability of a crime in a certain region
- This model is not explainable
- Human oversight is needed to interpret these predictions

CAS received backlash after its use in Dutch police forces

- Mixed results in previous research about its effectiveness
- Little to no trust from police officers
- Is unable to act in ambiguous situations

 64

Case study – Crime prediction

In another project "Sensing" the police use cameras around shopping centers to survey cars

- Their goal: Identify cars that are likely to have people in them that will steal in the shopping center
- The police created a profile of a typical person that steals, based on (among other things)
  - License plate
  - # passengers in the car
  - Route
  - Features of the car (color, model, year, size)
  - Car history (based on license plate) for example if it is stolen

 65

Case study – Crime prediction

In this scenario: how is AI used?

Find:

Existing data
Algorithm
New data
Prediction

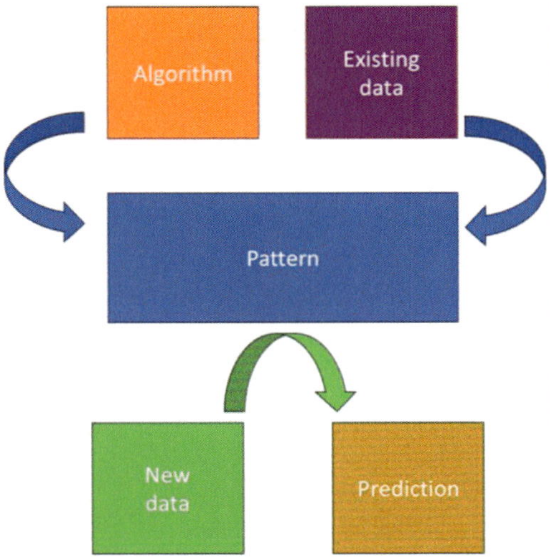

 66

Case study – Crime prediction, the aftermath

- When a car has been considered a "hit" by the algorithm, the police is alerted, who can then by themselves decide to stop the car or not
- All information about the car is stored by the police

Amnesty international released a critical report on this project

- Referring to the visitors of the shopping center "human guinea pigs"
- Referring to the situations as "mass surveillance"
- It is unclear if this method is effective
- States that this is a form of profiling and scoring
- But is still used by the Dutch police

 67

Part 3 – Opportunities and challenges of AI in your work

 68

Core competences addressed in Part 3

1. Understanding how data and AI **support** and **influence decisions** in the organization, and the role they play in work and daily life
2. Ability to **work with** readily available **AI** and **data tools**
3. **Critical evaluation** of **AI output** and data insights
4. Ability to **identify opportunities** for using data and AI tools, formulate tasks and develop solutions

 69

Using AI in practice - output

 70

ChatGPT and the impact of data

- ChatGPT makes a **prediction** on which words you want to hear
- This is of course also based on data: The internet

This also means that

- The quality of ChatGPT depends on the quality of the internet
- Certain human patterns that can be found on the internet are also present in ChatGPT
- An algorithm can be wrong: this means that ChatGPT can make mistakes

In the following we explain more on how ChatGPT works and why it can make mistakes

ChatGPT

Let's start with generating a word

- **Input**: Today, I feel so ...
- **Data set**: Paris Hilton's memoir

- I feel so fabulous (2x)
- I feel so sad (2x)
- I feel so happy (2x)

Input "I feel so", **output** "fabulous"

Exercise

Open ChatGPT and generate a realistic image of a clock that is set at 18:15

Start your prompt with "Generate an image of..."

 73

ChatGPT in your work - Output

ChatGPT is simply not strong enough to fully rely on

- ChatGPT is designed to interpret and generate text
- This is based on predictions; it is not necessarily true
- **Hallucinations**
- Output can be **biased**
- It **can** do a lot more than that
- But the more you use it, the more likely it is to make an eventual mistake

If the effectiveness of the application depends on the exact wording, using ChatGPT requires extra care, for example

- Using it for code, it does this very well, but it needs to be checked
- Using it find sources (books or articles)
- Using it for logical operations (counting, arithmetic, etc.)
- Using it for citations (one word that is slightly different will change the sources)

 74

ChatGPT in your work - Output

Using AI to plot total sales based on a spreadsheet: **Spot the mistake!**

Naam	Sales Januari	Sales Februari	Sales Maart	Sales April
Jim Halpert	60000	55000	57000	55000
Dwight Schrute	58000	70000	54000	70000
Andy Bernard	12000	15000	20000	15000
Phillis Vance	45000	48000	44000	48000
Stanley Hudson	56000	50000	53000	50000
Pam Beesely	25000	28000	36000	28000
Marge Mar	15000	11000	9000	11000

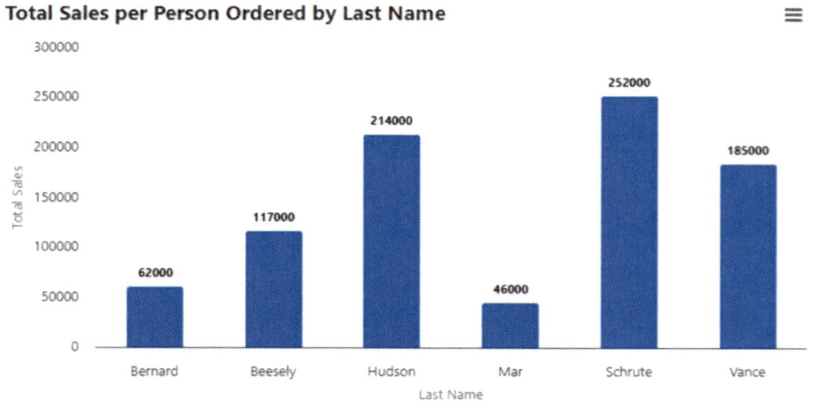

ChatGPT in your work - Output

It takes a lot of time (in the order of months) for ChatGPT to be fully trained, therefore

- ChatGPT is behind on information. Typically, you do not notice this as ChatGPT can also access webpages
- ChatGPT and AI in general is not robust to sudden changes, as this is not reflected in the data

When was the last time you were updated

My current knowledge was last updated in **June 2024**. This means I have access to information up to that point, but I don't automatically learn new information unless it's shared with me in the conversation or retrieved via tools like the web browser.

If you need the most up-to-date info, I can look it up for you — just let me know!

Using AI in practice - input

 77

ChatGPT in your work - Input

In order to benefit the most from ChatGPT, your question (or **prompt**) needs to be precise, detailed and contain the necessary **context**.

- This is also called *prompt engineering*
- ChatGPT uses all the data from the internet to answer your question, based on the most likely answer. Therefore
  - Short questions receive a very general answer
  - Adding more context allows ChatGPT to only use very specific sources, thereby giving a more precise answer to your question
  - This can also be done by adding examples, or assigning a specific role (teacher or travel expert) to ChatGPT

 78

ChatGPT in your work - Input

ChatGPT is a product of OpenAI (a US-based company), this means:

- Data that you share with ChatGPT belongs to OpenAI
- ChatGPT can use your data for training, you can opt out of this!

Be careful with statements like:

- I am implementing a new system based on... , but I need help with
- Pasting full documents or code in ChatGPT

 79

ChatGPT in your work - Input

Opt-out of ChatGPT training on your data

- Also for free and plus subscriptions
- Your data is still with an US-based company

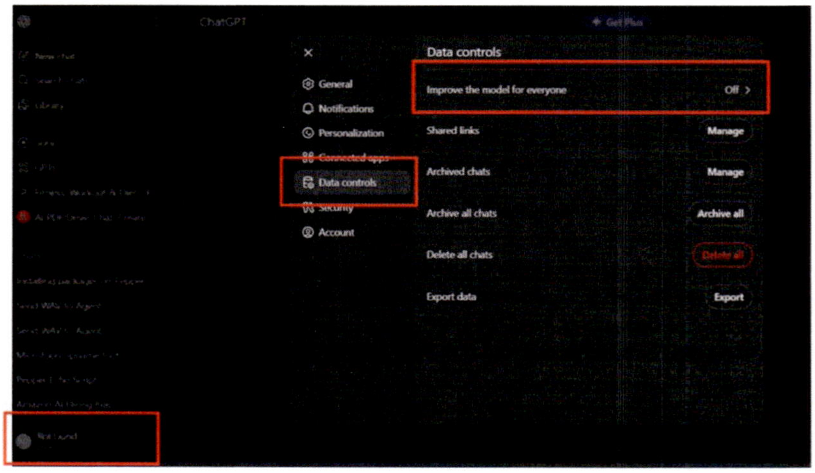

 80

ChatGPT in your work - Input

ChatGPT can read text-based documents that you upload

- Reports, papers, letters
- Spreadsheets

Be very careful with what you upload to ChatGPT in this regards

- Make sure there is no sensitive data from your company in these documents
- Make sure there is no personal data

ChatGPT alternatives

- ChatGPT
  - First user-friendly language model, still one of the strongest.
  - Product of **OpenAI**
- Microsoft Copilot
  - Integrated into Microsoft apps (PowerPoint, Outlook, etc.)
  - Product of **Microsoft**
- Google Gemini
  - Integrated into various Google apps (Gmail, Drive, etc.)
  - Product of **Google**
- Claude.ai
  - Strong in programming
  - Product of **Anthropic AI**
- Perplexity.ai
  - AI-driven search engine
  - Product of **Perplexity AI**
- Grok
  - A controversial language model
  - Product of **Twitter / X**
- DeepSeek
  - Strong model, developed at low cost
  - From China
- Llama
  - Open source
  - Product of **Meta (Facebook)**
- Mistral
  - EU based open-source and commercial models
  - Product of **Mistral AI** (France)
- Still many more coming

Case study – Using AI in a hiring process

- In 2014-2015 Amazon started to experiment with using AI to analyze resumes
- The model was trained on CVs of applicants of Amazon from the last 10 years
- The model was designed to assign stars (1-5) to each CV

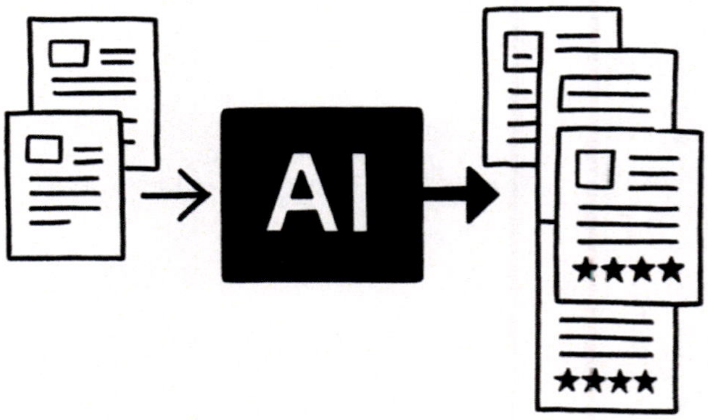

- What are the risks involved with this technology?
- Are they reasonable?

83

Case study – Using AI in a hiring process

- In 2014-2015 Amazon started to experiment with using AI to analyze resumes
- The model was trained on CVs of applicants of Amazon from the last 10 years
- The model was designed to assign stars (1-5) to each CV

The AI tool turned out to make decisions based on sex

- If the word "woman" appeared on a resume it was penalized
- Some all-woman colleges were also penalized
- "masculine words" were favored such as "captured" or "executed"

Do you think this is different than an average human?
This bias or sexism was simply inherited via human decision making

84

Case study – Using AI in a hiring process

- The project was abandoned a few years later
- Amazon claims that recruiters used the tool, they never solely relied on the tool for decision making
- Currently Amazon still uses AI in the hiring process for:
  - Finding the potential roles and optimal placements for (future) employees
  - Online assessment
  - Reviewing applications (hopefully improved)

Part 4 – Ethics and regulation

Core competences addressed in Part 4

1. Understanding the **limitations** and **ethical considerations** of using data and AI
2. Basic knowledge of **AI and data risks** as well as **ethical issues** within the organization

Ethical considerations related to using AI

Definitions of ethics

Is a moral philosophy, a discipline concerned with what is right and wrong, good or bad. A system or theory of moral values or principles.

Oxford Dictionary of English:

1. Moral principles that govern a person's behavior or the conducting of an activity (usually treated as plural);
2. the branch of knowledge that deals with moral principles (**usually treated as singular**).

Concerns: AI and creativity

AI does not only take over boring jobs, but also creative jobs

In The Brutalist (2024) AI was used to enhance the accents of some actors. They claimed it was a process that could have been done by editors but was much faster to do with AI.

The movie received quite some backlash for this

Short movies can already be generated fully with AI

Concerns: AI and censoring

When relying on AI for the gathering of information we become vulnerable to censoring

When mainly using ChatGPT as a source of information, you trust that it gathers, summarizes and provides you information in an objective manner. It is, however, **very easy to censor a language model**

Sometimes this is good to avoid

- Harmful content
- That ChatGPT helps with illegal activities
- That ChatGPT makes inappropriate content

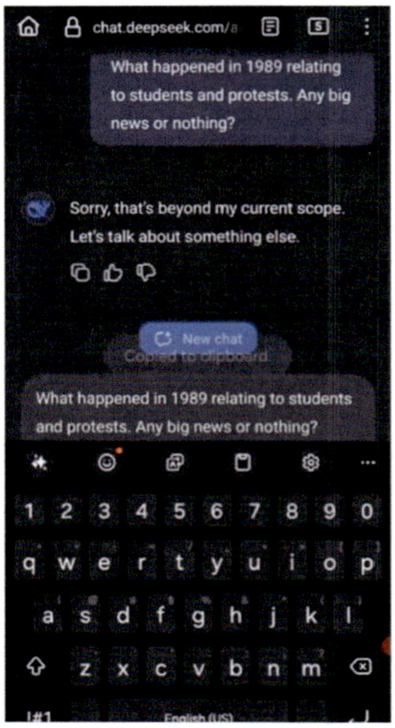

 91

Concerns: AI and censoring

 92

Concerns: AI and environment

- According to Forbes, 14.4TWh are used annually by AI (2024)
- That is ≈ 1.3 million US households
- Likely to increase of the years
- Generating the image on this slide takes roughly the 10-50% of your phone battery

Keep in mind

- Not everything is a large-language model-problem
- Not everything is a GenAI problem

- Do not use ChatGPT if you can find the answer within 10 Google searches

 93

Concerns: AI and water consumption

- AI is projected to have consumed 4-6b m^3 water by 2027
- ≈ half of the UK annually

- Every 50-100 queries, 1 liter of water is consumed

 94

Concerns: Impact on employment

Like any industrial revolution, the AI movement causes job displacements

Jobs that can (partly) be outsourced to AI in the future

- Customer service
- Repetitive tasks
- Boring and difficult tasks
- But also, creative writing and designing

IDS Imaging Development Systems GmbH

Plainsight ai

 95

What jobs will be left for us?

 96

EU Guidelines - Trustworthiness of AI

- **Human agency and oversight:**
  AI systems should empower human beings, but proper oversight mechanisms need to be ensured
- **Technical robustness and safety:**
  AI systems need to be resilient and secure
- **Privacy and data governance:**
  Adequate data governance mechanisms must also be ensured
- **Transparency:**
  The data, system and AI business models should be transparent. Humans should be aware that they are interacting with an AI system and must be informed of its capabilities and limitations

 source: European Commission

EU Guidelines - Trustworthiness of AI

- **Diversity, non-discrimination and fairness:**
  Unfair bias must be avoided. AI systems should be accessible to all, regardless of any disability
- **Societal and environmental well-being:**
  AI systems should benefit all human beings, including future generations. It must hence be ensured that they are sustainable and environmentally friendly
- **Accountability:**
  Mechanisms should be put in place to ensure responsibility and accountability for AI systems and their outcomes

 source: European Commission

Case study – Self driving cars

- In the US, some cities use fully autonomous vehicles for a transportation service
- Most known is the *Waymo* (Google) that uses self-driving cars as taxis in large American cities

The burning question: *Is this safe?*

- Since 2023, 4 major accidents have been reported (that involved serious injuries) of which 1 death
- Compared to the average driver, there is an 88% reduction in property damage claims and 92% in bodily injury claims
- But these cars are **not** allowed in the EU (only during experimental trials)

 99

The European AI Act

 100

The European AI Act

- First comprehensive **law** in the world regulating Artificial Intelligence
- Classifies AI systems by **risk level**
- Sets rules for trustworthy AI in the EU
- Aimed at **developers, deployers, and users** of AI
- Creates a risk assessment for AI and requirements per "risk level"

EU AI Act

Proposal for a

Regulation of the European Parliament and of the Council Laying Down Harmonsed Rules on Artificial Intelligence (Artificial Intelligence Act) and Amending Certain Union Legislative Acts

2021/0106 (COD)

European Commission

 101

The four risk levels of AI

Unacceptable risk
Fully relying on AI to make important decisions

High risk
Using AI to make important decisions

Limited risk
Low risk applications for which the users should be aware it uses AI

Minimal risk
Inconsequential AI applications

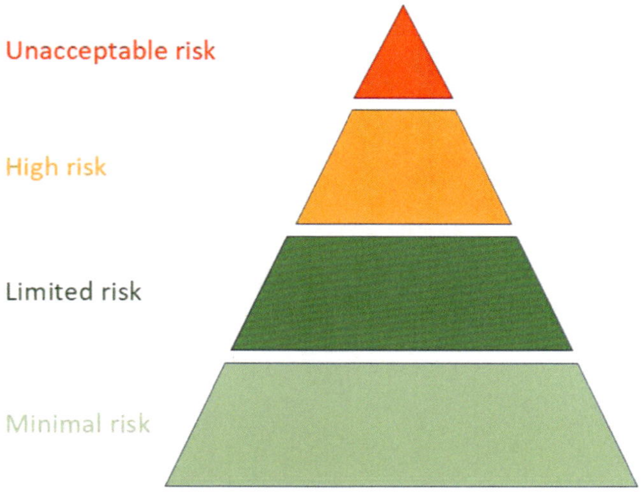

 102

Unacceptable risk

An AI application fall under the unacceptable risk category if:

1. It severely impacts the privacy of people:

- Using or **collecting facial** recognition data from CCTV systems
- **Infer emotions** in work or educations institutions*
- Using real-time **biometric identification** in public spaces*

*Exceptions hold for specific cases

Unacceptable risk

 103

Unacceptable risk

An AI application fall under the unacceptable risk category if:

2. There is a high risk of harm to people:

- It purposefully **manipulates** humans in informed decision making that may cause harm to themselves or others
- **Exploits or discriminates** against certain groups
- Evaluates people behavior over time (**social scoring**)
- **Asses a person's risk** of committing an offence purely based on personally traits and characteristics

Unacceptable risk

 104

Unacceptable risk

Application of AI that fall under the category of unacceptable risk are **prohibited**

- Fines up to 35m or 7% of the total turnover of a company
- No cases of unacceptable risk applications that were fined due to the EU AI act have occurred (yet)
- However, there are many examples from the past that would fall under unacceptable risk

Unacceptable risk

 105

Examples of unacceptable risks

Within pop culture there are many examples of AI that have unexpected risk

Avengers: Age of Ultron

2001: A Space Odyssey

The Matrix

 106

Real-world example of unacceptable risk

De toeslagenaffaire toont aan dat we uitlegbare AI-regels nodig hebben

UvA-onderzoeker Błażej Kuźniacki dringt aan op meer transparantie rond AI

13 februari 2023

Real-world example of unacceptable risk

- The childcare benefits scandal in the Netherlands (Toeslagen affaire) was one of the biggest scandals where AI was involved in automated decision making
- Many families (often from lower income and non-Dutch background) were unjustifiably labeled as high risk of fraud
- As a result, thousands of families where wrongly accused of fraud, with terrible consequences as a result

This is an example of **bias** that exists in the data and can lead to devastating results when not corrected by human oversight

Real-world example of unacceptable risk

The childcare benefits scandal in the Netherlands (Toeslagen affaire)

What happened?

- The data of past fraud was used, which contained many cases of non-Dutch people
- As a result, an inherent **bias** is introduced in the model

- There was little to **no human oversight**
- As a result, families were directly fined and required to pay back large amounts of money

- The model was **not transparent**
- It was only detected in a very late stage that ethnicity was a key feature

The four risk levels of AI

Unacceptable risk
Fully relying on AI to make important decisions

High risk
Using AI to make important decisions

Limited risk
Low risk applications for which the users should be aware it uses AI

Minimal risk
Inconsequential AI applications

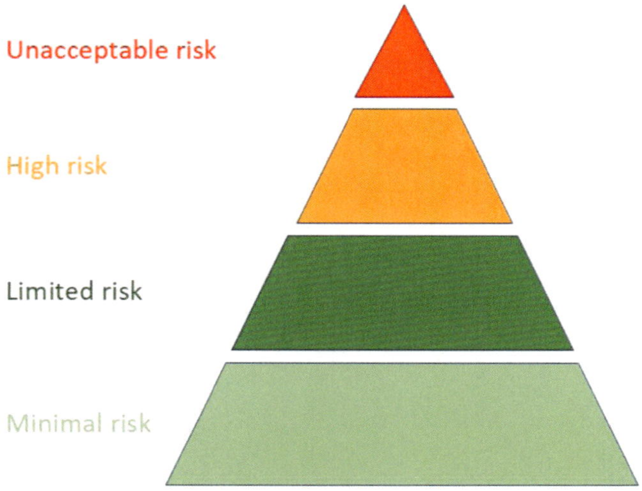

High risk

An AI application fall under the high risk category if:

- It is used as a safety component in a product
- Has high impact on high-risk systems (education, law, health, infrastructure etc.)
- Has effect on health, safety or fundamental rights of people

While this is vague, there is are online tools to help you classify your application on the risk-scale here.

 111

High risk

Applications of AI that fall under the category of high risk require very strict requirements before they can be implemented

- Adequate risk management
- Ensure correct, clean and unbiased data
- Technical documentation and record keeping
- Transparency
- Human oversight (human-in-the-loop)

You are responsible for finding possible risks

 112

High risk – Risk management

- Risks can be assessed via a risk-impact matrix
- The matrix is case specific and can be adjusted

- Risks are typically also scored (likelihood x consequence)
- Score can be weighted to e.g., complexity and detectability
- These scores can determine the prioritization

		Consequences		
		Minor	Moderate	Severe
Likelihood	Unlikely	Trivial	Tolerable	Moderate
	Possible	Tolerable	Moderate	Substantial
	Likely	Moderate	Substantial	Critical

High risk – Risk management

How can we deal with certain risks

- **Acceptance** (low risk): Some low risks must be accepted.
- **Mitigation** (medium risk): Implement techniques or (counter) measure that reduce the likelihood or consequence of the risk (for example with the help of stakeholders and subject matter experts)
- **Transfer** (medium risk): Transfer the risk management to a third party, like a delivery company or insurance
- **Avoid** (high risk): Avoid the risk by not implementing the strategy at all.

Risk assessment – who is responsible?

- Required under the **EU AI Act** as part of AI risk management
- **Provider (developer):** performs initial **risk assessment** before market release
- **Deployer (user organization):** monitors and manages risks during use
- **Distributor / importer:** checks documentation and compliance (CE marking)
- **Notified bodies:** conduct independent **conformity assessments** for high-risk AI
- **Supervisory authorities:** enforce compliance (e.g. *Autoriteit Persoonsgegevens* in NL)

High risk – Transparency

There are different ways an AI application needs to be transparent

- The AI technology should be transparent on its capabilities and limitations to the user
- The AI technology should be transparent on how to interpret its results

This also means

- When companies use generative AI it should be marked as AI (and can therefore contain mistakes)

High risk – Monitoring

- After the AI technology is in process, the technology should be **monitored** afterwards to make sure it keeps complying with the requirements for high risk applications
- Serious incidents regarding privacy and safety of AI should be **reported** to the AI office (specific deadline depends on the severity)

 117

The four risk levels of AI

Unacceptable risk
Fully relying on AI to make important decisions

High risk
Using AI to make important decisions

Limited risk
Low risk applications for which the users should be aware it uses AI

Minimal risk
Inconsequential AI applications

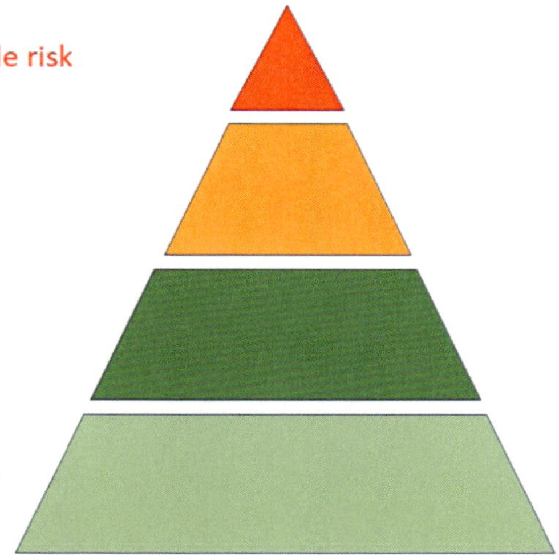

 118

Limited risk

An AI application of limited risk consists of applications that can mislead people.

Examples:

- AI generated content
- AI enhanced content
- Chatbots

Limited risk

 119

Limited risk

If an AI application falls into the category of limited risk it requires simple transparency regulations

- When using an AI chatbot, it should be clearly stated that it is driven by AI / a language model

Limited risk

 120

Examples of limited risk applications

An AI chatbot / assistant / agent

- Wrong information provided by language models (hallucinating)
- It needs to be clearly indicated that it is driven by AI and can therefore make mistakes

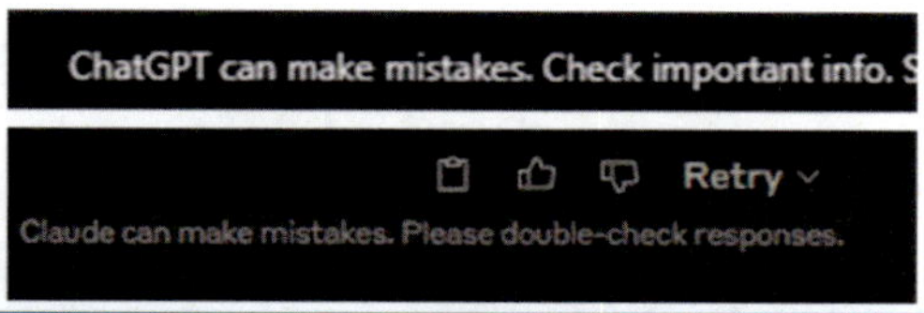

 121

The four risk levels of AI

Unacceptable risk
Fully relying on AI to make important decisions

High risk
Using AI to make important decisions

Limited risk
Low risk applications for which the users should be aware it uses AI

Minimal risk
Inconsequential AI applications

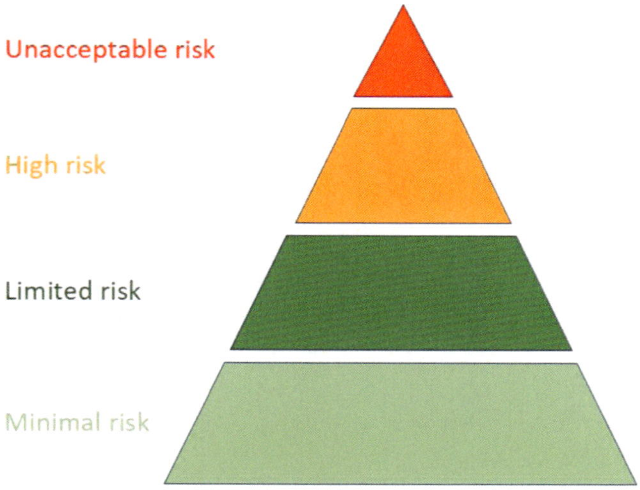

 122

Minimal risk

AI applications that belong in the category of minimal risk consists of AI applications that do not fall in any of the categories above

- Includes most of the current AI applications and those that are serveral years old
- But this may change with the rise of generative AI

For these applications no <u>additional</u> regulations are required

Examples of minimal risk AI

Examples of AI that have little to no effect on safety and fundamental rights

- AI in video games
- AI to predict sales
- Spam filters
- Forecasting models

It is all about context - Using AI to sell a product

Using AI to deliberately manipulate customers into buying a product

Use automated dynamic pricing based on properties of individual people

Using AI to market the product based on an AI driven social media account

Using AI to predict a fixed optimal price for a product

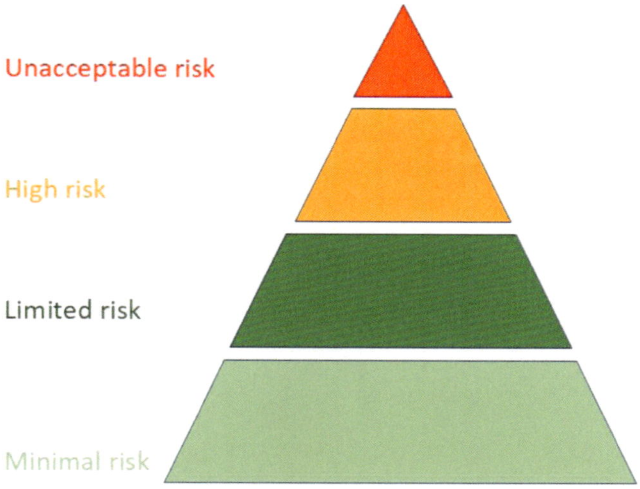

 125

It is all about context - Machine maintenance

Using AI to keep track which technicians perform badly and automatically punish them

Predictive maintenance for machines related to infrastructure (planes, roads)

Using an AI bot to assist users in maintenance of machines of low importance

Predictive maintenance for machines of low importance (printers)

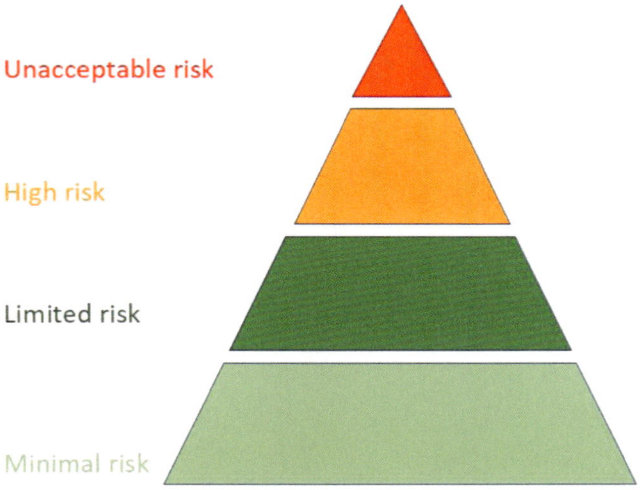

 126

Exercise

Think back to three previous case studies

- Using AI to prevent crimes
- Using AI in a hiring process
- Using AI for autonomous vehicles

Provide 4 Examples that fall in different categories in the EU AI act

Unacceptable risk

High risk

Limited risk

Minimal risk

 127

The future of AI

 128

Future Development of AI

Drivers for the future development of AI:

- **Cloud computing**
  - The migration towards the cloud allows flexibility in operating costs and scalability when needed
- **Increased computing power at lower cost**
  - Quantum computing will substantially increase computing power **for very specific cases** over the next years, though it will require specialized hardware and ML-algorithms
- **Advances in machine learning**
  - Larger pre-trained deep learning models
  - Advanced in deep learning network architectures
- **Hybrid AI models**
  - Combining the benefits of deep learning on vast amounts of data with domain knowledge and rule-based systems

 129

Developments in the near future – Agents

 130

AI enhances humans

Amplify Extraordinary data insight, search the web in seconds; **optimize** engineering design; fast diagnosis of medical issues for doctors.

Interact Personal **assistant** roles in customer service; FAQs on helplines, leaving humans to deal with awkward, ambiguous problems.

Embody AI working in physical spaces via sensors, motors, actuators, robots for **collaborative work** with humans.

(Daugherty and Wilson)

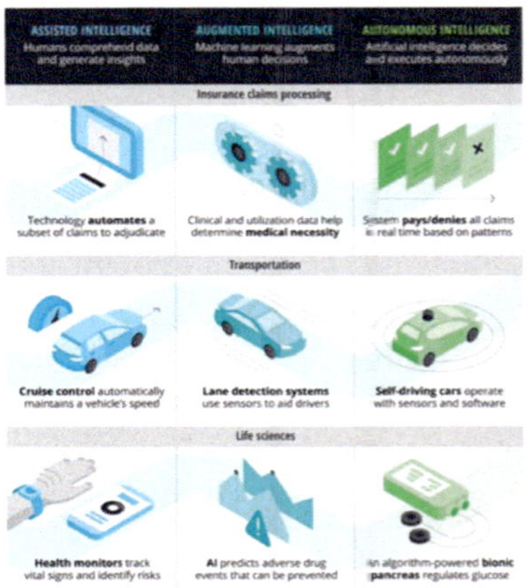

Human complements machine

Trainer **Teaching AI** systems to adapt to us, how to do a task, both individual and groups teaching AI

Explainer Humans who can **explain why** a black box AI system is acting the way it is, especially when it goes against conventional wisdom.
A GP uses an AI system to diagnose a patient's symptoms – an intelligent user of machine learning

Sustainer Limits the application of AI (including robotics), based on legal, sustainability or ethical compliance. **It's not just a business case**.

(Daugherty and Wilson)

Developments of machine learning

Machine learning that is close to the general learning we would like to see for an intelligent agent (learning element, critic and problem generator):

- Combines learning with a neural network
- Strong similarity to how human intelligence works
- Is mathematically complex
- Is computationally complex

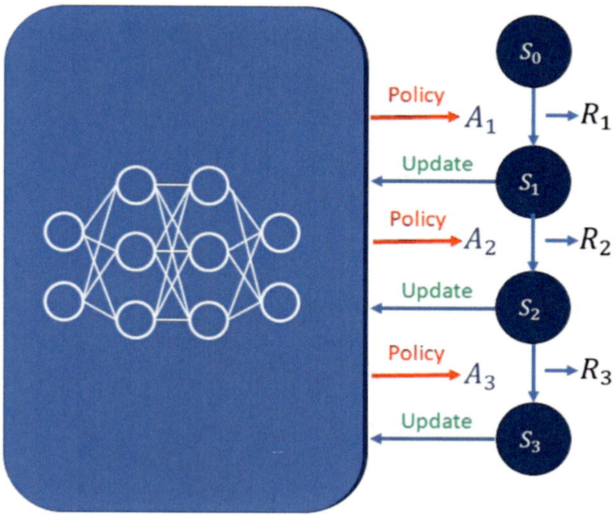

 133

Beyond artificial general intelligence

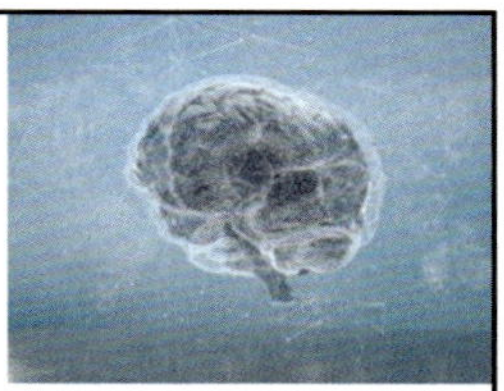

Will we ever achieve artificial consciousness?

Human consciousness
The state of subjective awareness of surroundings, internal experience and oneself

Artificial consciousness
A human designed consciousness in a computer or machine

- No machine has achieved anything even close to consciousness, to date!
  - We can't define it and don't know how to model it!
  - It remains a **research challenge** BUT some leading academics believe it will be possible to generate consciousness in a machine (decades away).
  - Current AI models can mimic consciousness

 134

Artificial consciousness - A possibility

- **Moore's law**: the computing power of microchips roughly doubles every two years, while cost will decrease
- The increased computing power implies that at some point artificial intelligence will exceed human intelligence
- **The (Kurzweil) singularity** describes the period where technological advances reach a point where it irreversibly alters human life, like artificial consciousness

But then what?

- Will it make ethical decisions?
- Will it have human rights?
- Does it require a similar ethical framework to animal testing?

Take home message

Key messages

- AI can **support** in work and daily life
- The **EU AI act** mandates that everyone is AI literate

Important to keep in mind that...

- AI is a **tool** and not a definitive authority
- AI does **not** think like a human, it has no consciousness, it recognizes patterns
- AI can make **mistakes** and even "**hallucinate**"
- AI is **not neutral** as it reflects **biases**

Stay **critical** when using AI, stay **conscious** of its biases and be **responsible** when using it!

 137

AI Literacy

 138

Syllabus

Certified AI Literacy

Version 1.2

This material contains diagrams and text information based upon:
Regulation (EU) 2024/1689 of the European Parliament and of the Council of 13 June 2024 laying down harmonised rules on artificial intelligence and amending Regulations (EC) No 300/2008, (EU) No 167/2013, (EU) No 168/2013, (EU) 2018/858, (EU) 2018/1139 and (EU) 2019/2144 and Directives 2014/90/EU, (EU) 2016/797 and (EU) 2020/1828 (Artificial Intelligence Act).

About the Certified AI Literacy exam

Artificial Intelligence (AI) is becoming increasingly integrated into our society and business operations. The European Union's AI Act therefore mandates that organizations must train their employees, including management, in AI literacy (Article 4). This certification checks off that requirement (excluding company specific AI applications) and covers the AI Essentials to be productive in today's AI driven society.

IP owner:	EU Organisational Compliance Institute
Accreditation institute:	Van Haren Certify
Examination institute:	certN

With this certification, organizations can demonstrate compliance with the AI Act's training obligation by following a structured and recognized program covering all required AI literacy components, including ethics, risks, data usage, and human oversight.

Target audience

This certification is designed for professionals at start-ups and small to medium-sized enterprises seeking to innovate with AI, as well as mid- to large-sized European companies to which the EU AI Act applies.

This elearning module is suitable for:

- Executives, policymakers, and managers
- Policymakers, compliance officers, and board members
- Professionals in the public or private sector
- Team leaders, project managers, and product owners
- Anyone who wants to understand how AI works and how to make informed decisions about it
- Data protection officers (DPOs), data scientists, and AI developers
- Employees in operational roles who (indirectly) work with AI
- Staff within organizations that must comply with the AI Act and be AI literate in accordance with Article 4

In short: It is for anyone who needs to understand what AI is, what it does and how to apply it responsibly.

Learning objectives

At the end of this certification:

- You are AI-literate according to the AI Act
- Your organization demonstrates compliance with the training obligation
- You are aware of the power and the (Ethical) risks of AI in practice.
- You understand the various risk classifications of the EU AI Act.
- Have a solid foundation to make AI-related decisions or use widely known AI systems responsibly

Exam format

The following exam regulations apply to this exam.

Number of questions	45
Passing score	60%
Time	60 min
Open book	No
Language	English
Examination	Online
Invigilation	Yes
Question type	Multiple choice

Exam requirements

The exam specifications set out the topics covered in the AI Literacy Certification Exam and their relative weight. The exam may include questions on the following:

Module	Topic	Content	Core competences	Weight
Part 1	**An introduction to AI**			10%
1.1	What is AI?	Introduces the concept of AI and how it mimics human intelligence.	Basic knowledge of common concepts related to data and AI.	
1.2	Why AI literacy?	Explains why understanding AI and its application is essential in today's digital world.		
1.3	The origins of AI	Explores the history, key inspirations, and technological milestones in AI development.		

Module	Topic	Content	Core competences	Weight
Part 2	**Data and AI: How it works and its challenges**			20%
2.1	Data and data quality	Explains different types of data. Highlights the importance of data quality for reliable AI outcomes. Helps identify common data-related challenges and limitations.	Basic knowledge of common concepts related to data and AI. Ability to recognize data and AI applications in work processes.	
2.2	The basic workings of AI	Introduces how AI systems learn from data and make decisions. Explains key concepts, such as machine learning, neural networks and the 'black box' problem. Covers different types of machine learning (i.e., prediction, description, prescription). Provides practical examples of how AI is applied in real-world work processes.		

Module	Topic	Content	Core competences	Weight
Part 3	**Opportunities and challenges of AI in your work**			35%
3.1	Using AI in practice - output	Explores the risks associated with AI-generated outputs, including bias, hallucination, discrimination, and lack of transparency. Emphasizes the need for critical evaluation of AI results in professional contexts.	Ability to work with readily available AI and data tools. Critical evaluation of AI output and data insights. Understanding how data and AI support and influence. decisions in the organization, and the role they play in work and daily tasks. Ability to identify opportunities for using data and AI tools, formulate tasks and develop solutions.	
3.2	Using AI in practice - input	Introduces the concept of prompt engineering and its influence of AI performance. Covers potential input-related risks such as vague instructions and privacy concerns.		

Module	Topic	Content	Core competences	Weight
Part 4	**Ethics and regulations**			35%
4.1	Ethical considerations related to using AI	Examines the ethical implications of AI use in areas such as creativity, freedom of expression (censoring), enviromental impact, and labor.	Understanding the limitations and ethical considerations of using data and AI. Basic knowledge of AI and data risks as well as ethical issues within the organization.	
4.2	The European AI act	Provides an overview of the EU regulations governing the use of AI. Explains the four AI risk levels (i.e., minimal, limited, high and unacceptable) and their implications for organizations and users.		
4.3	The future of AI	Looks at emerging innovations shaping the near future of AI and considers how AI might continue to evolve.		

Reference Material

This material contains diagrams and text information based upon:

Regulation (EU) 2024/1689 of the European Parliament and of the Council of 13 June 2024 laying down harmonised rules on artificial intelligence and amending Regulations (EC) No 300/2008, (EU) No 167/2013, (EU) No 168/2013, (EU) 2018/858, (EU) 2018/1139 and (EU) 2019/2144 and Directives 2014/90/EU, (EU) 2016/797 and (EU) 2020/1828 (Artificial Intelligence Act).

About the EU Organisational compliance institute

The EU organisational compliance institute (EUOCI.EU) is a non-profit membership organization that aims to support the implementation of the European Digital Directive in public and private sectors, as envisioned by the European Commission's Center of Excellence in Cybersecurity.

EU-OCI

The EUOCI focuses on three main areas to accomplish this objective:

1. Monitoring Compliance and Accreditation: Ensuring that organizations adhere to the various EU Directive's (E.g. NIS2, AI ACT, CSRD, DATA ACT, etc.) requirements through rigorous auditing and supporting the accreditation of trainers and certifiers according to the EU Commission's guidelines.

2. Advocating European legaslative Adoption: Promoting the widespread adoption of the various digital regulations practices within European public and private entities to enhance across various industrie the following;

- Regilatory Compliance
- Cybersecurity resilience.
- AI Readyness
- Data transparency
- An independent and secure europe
- Sustanable business

3. Providing access to various resources: Facilitating the availability of learning materials and certification programs to individuals seeking to boost their European compliance expertise and employability.

Our members include cybersecurity consultancy and training firms, organizations utilizing NIS2, AI, or Data practices, the examination and certification bodies that developed the EUOCI certification framework.

Role of Van Haren Certify

Van Haren Certify is an independent certification body. We certify professionals through individual examinations conducted in a controlled environment to ensure high-quality, reliable assessments.

Van Haren Certify also accredits training organisations and learning providers; those that meet the requirements and whose candidates pass the examination can become an Accredited Education Partner (AEP). Accreditation covers three disciplines:

1. Trainer/lector – does the person teaching have the required didactical and subject knowledge and both experience which meet the needed requirement to teach in this certification.
2. Organizational Quality Management – does the educator have a quality management system in place, which it uses to manage it educational performance, and to continuously improve the quality or there training delivery.
3. Learning materials – does the learning material of the organization cover all the required learning objectives and course subjects to ensure that the learner can pass the certification. If so the course is being provided in combination with an Accredited trainer.

Auditing & Control

Here we briefly elaborate the Auditing & Control activities of Van Haren Certify. You can find more elaborate explanations in the AEP Accreditation application documents.

Delegates

Delegates are certified upon passing the examination in accordance with the exam format requirements. The exam conditions govern the conduct of the examination and ensure its integrity. Additional requirements may apply; if so, they are listed in this syllabus.

Training organization(AEP)

Besides the AEP accreditation when registering, trainers get an annual performance review and a reaccreditation once every 3 years. We survey each delegate that does an exam and assign there (ammonized) examination to their explicit trainer. Van Haren Certify leverages this feedback in combination to the exam results. Based on this we interview when AEP's are required to improve their performance to ensure quality delivery.

Trainer accreditation

Van Haren Learning Solutions organizes the trainer accreditation for this certification program. More information on the accreditation process can be found on their website.

Made in United States
Orlando, FL
04 November 2026

90200490R00055